home
Sweet
HOME

MARY ENGELBREIT'S

home
Sweet
HOME

A Journey Through Mary's Dream Home

Mary Engelbreit
Text by Patrick Regan

Andrews McMeel
Publishing

Kansas City

M∃ MARY ENGELBREIT

www.maryengelbreit.com

Library of Congress Cataloging-in-Publication Data

Engelbreit, Mary.
    Mary Engelbreit's home sweet home : a journey through Mary's dream home.
      p. cm.
    ISBN 0-7407-4512-3
      1. House furnishings. 2. Interior decoration. I. Title: Home sweet home. II. Title.
    TX311.E6423 2004
    747-dc22   2004047731

Designer: Stephanie R. Farley
Editor: Polly S. Blair
Writer: Patrick Regan
Stylist: Heidi Adams
Production Manager: Elizabeth Nuelle

For Phil—
"My Home Is In Your Eyes"

—Abraham Lincoln

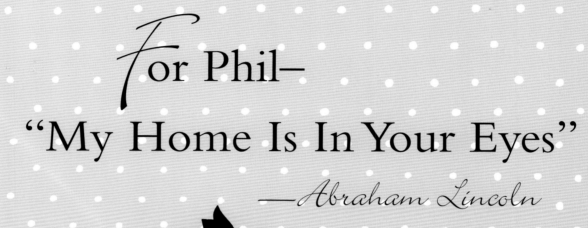

Acknowledgments

Heidi Adams

Jackie Ahlstrom

Alexa Anderson

David Arnold

Stephanie Barken

John Bessler

Polly Blair

Mary Engelbreit

Stephanie Farley

Mikayla

Charlotte Nenninger

Elizabeth Nuelle

Irene Pappas

John Smallwood

Ella Stewart

Nancy Yount

Contents

I'll confess—I've always had a soft spot for stories with unabashedly happy endings. The book you're now holding tells a story very close to my heart. It's about my love affair with a house, and how—through luck, perseverance, imagination, and hard work—the house of my dreams finally became a reality for my family and me.

Introduction

I've always lived in my hometown of St. Louis, but my family and I have done more than our share of moving. Why bother? I love houses. I love the challenge of digging in, tearing out, experimenting, and turning a house into our unique home. About the time I'd finish with one house, I'd get the urge to start fresh somewhere else. That was my continuing story, with chapters never-ending . . . or so I thought.

Through all of these moves (for the record, there have been six over the past two-and-a-half decades or so), there was always one house in town that captivated me. I had admired it for longer than I could remember and had always told my husband, "That's where I want to live."

Unfortunately, someone else already called the house home. As with any good story, the one in this book has twists and turns and moments of anxiety (including one heart-wrenching day when the house of my dreams was sold to someone else!). Life has a funny way of working out, and remember, I wouldn't be telling this story if it didn't have a happy ending.

But I'm getting ahead of myself. Turn the page, and we'll start this story at the beginning!

Welcome to my *Home Sweet Home*. I'm so glad you decided to stop by.

"The house would play
peekaboo with Mary as she
drove to her studio."

First glimpse

When this attraction first took hold,
Mary Engelbreit cannot say. Fifteen years
ago? Twenty? For certain, her enchantment
with this house had been growing for a long,
long time.

First glimpsed through dense leaves, set
back on a heavily wooded lot, the house
would play peekaboo with Mary as she drove
to her studio down a shady lane through one
of St. Louis's older suburbs.

In the winter months, when the trees
were bare, the house gave up more of its
secrets. A steep-pitched, shingled roof. Old-
fashioned, multi-paned windows. A winding,
tree-canopied drive. The more Mary saw,
the more she liked. Intrigue grew to flat-out
attraction. Mary Engelbreit was smitten.

The object of Mary's affection was not imposing or ostentatious. It was big enough for a family, but cozy-looking. Impossible as it seemed, it was a cottage in the woods—right there in the city.

Mary wasn't alone in her admiration for this storybook house. In fact, just two years after it was built in 1923, it was included in a book titled *Missouri's*

And while that may have been the first public appreciation of the home, it would be far from the last. While under the care of a previous owner, the house was featured in *Better Homes and Gardens* and other shelter magazines of note. When Mary launched her own home décor magazine in 1996, the cottage in the woods was

"People who see it immediately say, 'This is your house! This is the house you were meant to live in.' It's true. It looks like a little seven dwarves' house."

Contribution to American Architecture. Having been passed along with the house through all previous owners, the heavy book now sits on Mary's coffee table, open to a picture of the house on page 258. The trees are a bit thinner in the old black-and-white photo, but the house's profile is instantly recognizable.

among the first places Mary wanted her photographers and editors to feature.

"I had always loved the outside of the house, but had never seen the inside," she remembers. The magazine photo-shoot gave her the perfect entrée. When she finally did cross the threshold, she wasn't disappointed.

"The owner at the time had an excellent sense of style, and the house was decorated beautifully," recalls Mary.

Of course, Mary couldn't suppress her natural creative impulse to mentally recast the well-appointed rooms in her own style. "I have to admit that it was my first instinct," she says. "It was beautiful, but it wasn't what I would've done." But Mary would have to be satisfied with an imaginary redo for now. The lovely home's owners (who were not, incidentally, named Grumpy, Sneezy, or Bashful) were quite happily ensconced.

Mary's first opportunity to own her dream house came 1998. The owner of the house, whom Mary had become friendly with after various photo-shoots, called her out of the blue to say that the house would soon be available. The timing couldn't have been worse. "We had just built a house from the ground up," Mary remembers. "I was sick about it, but we had just moved in, and I had to tell her, 'I can't do it.'" As Mary lamented, another buyer quickly snapped up the coveted prize.

To make matters worse, the house that Mary's family had recently finished constructing seemed somewhat less than a perfect fit. Mary seems almost apologetic toward the house when she discusses it now. "It was a really nice house," she says, "but . . . I like older houses. I couldn't get used to a house where all the windows went up and down

and everything actually worked. It was a foreign environment to me."

But, in truth, two moves in four years had left Mary and family with a severe case

of relocation fatigue. Mary laughs about this now, remembering that Phil had sworn at the time that he would never move again. They settled in to the new house and eventually Mary managed to recover from the sting of missing out on her dream house. Real estate sages love to recite the mantra "Location, location, location," but just as often, it's "Timing, timing, timing" that counts.

Well, as any fan of fairy tales knows, the darkest hour comes right before dawn. For Mary, dawn broke the day she received an unexpected phone call. The family that had bought the house just over a year before had decided to move on. Mary's dream home was again within her grasp, and this time—feeling that destiny was truly pounding on the door—she didn't hesitate.

"It was as if the house was trying to be sold to us," said Mary. "I was thrilled, of course, but there was also a feeling of resignation, like, 'Oh fine, we'll buy it.'"

As for Phil—well, this fairy tale still has a resident Prince Charming. Up to this point, he had never seen the house, but Mary never doubted that it would win him over too. She was right. All it took was one visit for Phil to rescind his earlier proclamation. "We drove up the driveway," remembers Mary, "and the second he saw it, he said, 'Okay.'"

That's not the end of this happy story, of course. It's really just the beginning. Five years on, the nest-hopping artist has settled in and has no intention of moving again—no time soon, at least. She's steadily gone about the business of transforming the home into one that reflects her family's lifestyle, her humor, her attitude, and her art.

No home of Mary's is ever
truly finished, and yes,
she reserves the right
to reshuffle furnishings on a whim,
but no matter how Mary
tucks and tweaks the décor,
the overwhelming feelings in this home
are always warmth and welcome.
Home is, after all,
where the heart is.
And the heart of this home
pulses in every room.

Cottage in the Woods

The house sits on a two-acre lot that feels larger for the mature forest that surrounds it. Though in one of St. Louis's older, "close-in" suburbs—only about a 15-minute drive from downtown—it has the feel of a quiet, slightly slouchy country estate. It's easy to miss the narrow, tree-crowded driveway, curling right, then left, just enough to obscure the view of the other end. Once around the bend, the house is revealed suddenly. With its steep-pitched roof, copious multi-paned windows, and Old World charm, it looks like it was plucked from one of Mary's drawings. It's only on second glance that you're likely to notice the cherry-shaped cutouts on the wooden shutters. There's no doubt, now, that you've entered Mary's world.

"*There are not many houses*
that look like this in St. Louis," says Mary.
And she should know.
She's spent decades poking around estate sales
and open houses all over the city.
(Few people have as consistent
and comfortable a relationship with
their real estate agent as Mary.)
"It's an unusual style for the area.
I believe that architecturally it's considered
Cotswold style. But I call it storybook style."
Engelbreit style would also be appropriate.

$\mathcal{V}$isitors to Mary's storybook house are likely to be greeted by the smallest of hosts—granddaughter Mikayla usually wins the race to the door. The seven-foot-tall, carved wooden doors (facing page) once graced a home in England. They were brought back by a previous owner and added to the house during a renovation in the 1980s. Though Mikayla may think the low doorknobs were positioned just for her, this idiosyncrasy is owed to the fact that the house on which the door originally hung stood at the top of steep steps.

If best friends come in by way of the back door, there's good reason everyone feels the spirit of friendship at Mary's house. The orientation of the house, and indeed the address, was actually switched by a previous owner, so the main entrance is now through the back. The original front of the house is shown on page 20.

A dry-stack stone wall snakes across the backyard, marking the transitional area between cultivated chaos and full-blown forest (facing page). Beyond the wall, a weathered picket fence signifies not the end of the property line, but the end of Mary's comfort zone. "There's a little path that leads to the original water well for the property," she says. "But I got a tick the last time I wandered around back there, so I've never been out there again."

Tender touches turn up everywhere in Mary's world. At right, a cast concrete fairy alights on a mosaic-tiled chair found at a flea market.

A wren-ready cottage (left), complete with daisy-filled flower boxes, proudly flies the flag. The birdhouse was made by Jesse Hickman.

This exquisite garden gate once hung in an old cemetery in England. The home's previous owner found it at an antique shop on an overseas visit, and when it was time to move decided that the gate should stay with the house.

A cluster of paper lanterns illuminates the backyard gazebo (right). Just a short walk down the flagstone path from the swimming pool, the gazebo offers genteel respite from the sun on a warm summer's afternoon and an enchanting hideaway on mild evenings. Though it looks like it's been there since the Truman administration, the gazebo was one of Mary and Phil's additions to the property.

A home of her own Under the shade of two century-old oak trees, Mikayla's playhouse offers all the comforts of home. Complete with gardens and a white picket fence and arbor, Mikayla's make-believe *maison* mirrors Mary's home on a preschool scale. Even the steep-roofed birdhouses hanging nearby echo the home's distinctive style (facing page).

*"I'm so fortunate—
to get to do what I love for a living
and to do it in a comfortable,
beautiful setting surrounded by family."*

*Mary's sister Alexa once said, "Mary draws life, and life keeps happening." To ensure that moments of
inspiration aren't lost, Mary's tools of the trade (for a quick sketch, at least) are never far away (above).*

*Just steps outside the back door, the irresistible patio nook pictured at left catches foliage-filtered morning
sun, offering a splendid spot for a quiet cup of coffee and a quick look at the day's news.*

A faded arched gate is all that's visible from the street of Mary's secluded domain (facing page). The hanging planter was received as a Christmas gift— Mary changes out the flowers each season . . . well, most of the time.

Mary has never professed to having much of a green thumb, and though she'd love to claim responsibility for the flourishing gardens surrounding her home, she gives credit where it is due. Gardener Julie Songer is the primary caretaker for the extensive and in many cases, rare specimens of flora that thrive on the property. "The landscaping was pretty spectacular when we bought this place," recalls Mary.

Mary lavishes most of her personal attention on the striking perennial garden right outside the kitchen's big bay window. But since moving in, they've learned that the surrounding woods hold secret gardens of their own. An expert from St. Louis's renowned Missouri Botanical Garden planted rare specimens of ferns and other plants among the mature trees. Julie is gradually transplanting many of these closer to the house to assure that they are not lost to the outer wilds of the property.

Even a brief pause to rest should
be worth taking now.

Living Room

Step through the antique, English double doors into Mary Engelbreit's house and, at first glance, all seems fairly conventional. A sideboard cabinet in the entryway holds a stack of mail, a set of keys, a pair of sunglasses, and other evidence of a busy household. Take a few steps more, however, and the surprises begin. The eight-foot-high ceiling gives way, and the room suddenly and dramatically opens into an airy space of outdoorsy proportions. Open to the rafters, sunlight filters in through skylights directly above and big windows on three sides of the room. Pale greens and creams dominate the décor, gently reasserting the soft, relaxing feel of the large room.

A cream-colored, slip-covered
couch backed up by a distressed,
light emerald sofa table
divides the room into roughly a third,
helping to keep conversations
on an intimate scale.
The couch is positioned under the main
support beam of this open room,
heightening the natural feel of its location.
A big believer in slipcovers, Mary laughs
when asked if she swaps them out
to fit the season.
"That's a myth," she says.
"Nobody ever changes slipcovers."

You never know what you might find overhead in Mary's house. Aloft in the rafters, a miniature cold frame built out of salvaged wood trim houses vintage story books and dried flowers (left). Cast iron birds roost safely out of reach of granddaughter Mikayla's curious touch, and a few more green-roofed birdhouses echo the room's dominant accent color.

Standard fire screens weren't large enough to span the broad opening of the living room fireplace (facing page), so Mary improvised, using a section of iron garden fencing instead. With the gas-burning fireplace, flying sparks aren't an issue. Mary was charmed by the unusual fourplex birdhouse on the mantel, and its pale green roof made it a natural addition to the room. Vintage fabric and paper parasols dress up the cavernous fireplace when it's not in use.

Although this room is significantly larger than any single room in the family's previous home, Mary outfitted it with nary a stick of new furniture—although she did combine the contents of two other rooms to fill this one. Mary admits that it took considerable trial and error to find the right layout for the room. Her solution? Sitting areas oriented toward natural points of focus. There's a spacious conversation area in front of the wide, brick fireplace, another comfortable nook with overstuffed wing chairs and loveseat tucked in by the south-facing bay window, and another spot, great for reading or quiet conversation, on the edge of the room, just off the entry way. An unobtrusive wet bar in the northeast corner of the room makes the already obvious even more so . . . this is a great room for entertaining!

Warm welcome A reconditioned antique sideboard standing in the entryway (facing page) *is fanciful and functional. Mary bought it from a shop that specializes in combining separate old furnishings to achieve unique looking new pieces. The tray sitting in the middle is a handy spot for outgoing mail, car keys, and sunglasses. The three-tiered pastry tray* (below, right) *on the sideboard's shelf began life as "shiny, ugly brass" but once painted white by Mary became the perfect platform for an assortment of shells found on Florida beaches.*

*B*oth Mary and Phil have a tendency to be less than vigilant about keeping track of their eyeglasses. A quick tour around the house reveals Mary's solution—there are extra pairs everywhere . . . on her drawing table, next to her favorite reading chair, on Mikayla's bedside table, and next to her own bed . . . even she's not sure how many pairs are circulating throughout the house. Phil's folly is clip-on sunglasses. He loses a pair, buys a replacement, then finds the original (above, left).

1

2

3

inspiration

Mary's most recent collection/obsession started off innocently enough. Having purchased the fragile clowns *(right)* a decade ago at an antique store, she wanted to keep them protected from cats, kids, and clumsy adults. She dropped a vintage cloche over the top and liked the way that the enclosure seemed to freeze time and heighten the dramatic effect. Now she's always on the lookout for bell jars of all sizes and takes delight in grouping related, and sometimes seemingly incongruous items, artifacts, and photos under glass. "My collecting habits have changed over the years," says Mary. "It's not about the volume or even the rarity of the pieces. I like it when collections can tell little stories."

The fragility of these porcelain-faced clowns inspired Mary's first bell jar vignette *(2, 4)*.

In this cloche *(1)*, a silk butterfly is suspended above a picture of Mary as a young girl with her mother and father. She glued the photo onto a small plate and added buttons for a border. The bell jar at right *(5)* safeguards an even older photo of Mary's mother with her aunt and grandmother.

under glass

Mary created the vignette on the facing page *(3)* for her son, Evan. He made the metal "E" in a jewelry class.

4

5

The Golden Hour Late afternoon sunlight streams in through the living room's tall triple-hung, west-facing windows (facing page). The round, maple-topped game table is a genuine antique, "but I keep painting it, thus ruining the value," laughs Mary. Blown-glass hanging vases found during a trip to Vermont catch the light and cast spots of green about the room (above, left). Mary hung white wreaths (above, right) in the windows at Christmas, but liked the way they looked so left them up when the other ornaments came down.

Soft tones and softer seating create the perfect spot for a catnap or a teatime chat. Mary's inspirations are as far ranging as her sources. The floral seat cushions on the couch were fashioned from old drapes. The rug, like the rest in this room, was purchased at a tent sale at Home Depot. Two fanciful vintage birdcages lend a whimsical avian touch above the couch. Though she's never owned an actual bird, you'll rarely see an empty birdcage in Mary's house. Most are inhabited by realistically hand-created, felt and cotton batting birds that Mary guesses date from the 1920s. The specimen housed in the small cage on the opposite page is a rarer, painted cast iron model made long ago specifically as a birdhouse decoration.

Variations on a theme   Mary admits to being a chronic rearranger. The photos above and at right show how subtle changes to one area of the living room affect the overall mood and tone.

The two framed illustrations hanging to the left of the bay window are original watercolors from famed illustrator Johnny Gruelle's Raggedy Ann and Andy storybook series. Gruelle was one of Mary's favorite illustrators when she was a child and had a major influence on her style as an artist. The pieces have hung in Mary's various homes for nearly twenty years, but she reframed them in blue-green to complement the living room's color scheme.

Sun-dappled serenity
The southwest corner of the living room
radiates warmth in the afternoon light. The
living room's pale green and off-white color
palette was inspired by the vintage throw
pictured on the facing page.

Three of a kind

The complementary pieces of McCoy pottery
perched on the windowsill above were various estate
sale or antique store finds. They were chosen for their
shape, design, and color without regard for label or
value. "Collecting is an emotional experience
for me," Mary explains. "My only criterion
is if I like how something looks.
I operate from the heart, not the brain."

Mary is particularly fond of this throw (right)
because it is something of an anomaly—
such textiles are traditionally rendered in red and
white and are, in fact, often referred to as redwork.
They are rarely seen in green.

Residence of Marion Niedringhaus Ladue Road, St. Louis County
Built in 1925
Beverley T. Nelson, St. Louis, Architect

*T*he *1925 book,* Missouri's Contribution to American Architecture, *featuring a photograph of Mary's house circa 1923 (left), has been passed down with the house beginning with the house's original owners. Another one of Mary and Phil's former houses can also be found in the book as well as one of her studios, a converted Greek Orthodox church.*

Counterpoint

An alternative arrangement in the northwest corner shows the impact that a dash of additional color brings to the living room. A brown gingham wing back chair picks up the warm tones of the wide plank flooring, while various pale blue accessories complement the room's abundant soft greens. The daffodil decorated urn on the floor is actually a vintage chamber pot.

Stories of a lifetime Two cherished collections mingle effortlessly in this painted china cabinet. Mary has collected vintage baby plates for two decades, and antiquarian children's books have been a lifelong love. Many of the volumes in this cabinet originally belonged to Mary's maternal grandmother, Ann Estelle (yes, the namesake for Mary's own spunky little girl character). The well-loved books are cared for but not treated as museum pieces. Favorites are often pulled out at Mikayla's story time. Cinderella is a particular favorite. The top of the cabinet provides a safe haven for another collection, of marble busts. The collection began with the girl reading (far right). Ever since, Mary explains, her eye just seems drawn to them in shops. Apart from the small clowns in the foreground, all of the pieces depict sweet-faced children. "They have to be cute," she declares in true Engelbreit form.

This simple table lamp (right) got the Mary treatment with a bit of floral giftwrap around the candlestick and a beaded tassel.

The vaulted ceilings in the living room keep Mary thinking vertically. Bare real estate above the door to the screened-in porch was a perfect spot for this bird and botanical themed shelf (left) which charmed Mary at a furnishings store. "Every horizontal surface in my house is covered," says Mary with a laugh. "I have to have these little shelves around for the overflow." This one holds miniature topiaries from Michaels, a painted iron wreath, and a vintage clown walking toy.

A home of their own
A small shadow box (left)
provides the perfect spot for
little odds and ends that might
otherwise end up lost in the
back of a drawer somewhere.
Sharing the cozy confines are
miniature bird eggs, a tin-boxed
ink pad, a papier-mache
birdhouse, and flowers salvaged
from a favorite old hat.

From emerald to celadon, with countless values in
between, Mary's living room proudly wears many shades
of green. Mary winces at the notion of adhering to a
strict color palette, and even when creating a room with a
predominant décor color, like her living room, she allows
herself a broad range to work within. "People see a room
in my magazine and want to know exactly what color
I'm using," she explains. "Well, usually I don't even know
or care, and it really doesn't matter. There are thirty
different colors of green in this room. I just want to tell
people, 'Don't worry about it—pick a color and throw in
a bunch of stuff that agrees with it. It'll all go together.'
What I try to do in a room is create a mood. I'm not
trying to match everything."

Dining Room

The dark side of Mary Engelbreit? Well, hardly. But the formal dining room in Mary's home does employ a deeper, darker palette than her fans might guess. And while it may be the "most serious" room in the house, that's not to say it lacks spirit or flair.

In her dining room, Mary achieves old-fashioned elegance—but without a hint of pretense. To design this room she began with the wallpaper and added furnishings to taste. Don't bother looking for a matching dining set. "No, the buffet and the table don't match," she says, "and it doesn't matter. As long as things mix, they don't have to match."

"*One of the things
I love about this house is
that we really use every room.
Still, it's nice to have a room
that's kind of set aside
for special occasions.*"

The room's palette of tans, browns, and greens was inspired by Mary's transferware collection (some of which sits on top of the mantle). Because the room is used mainly for special-occasion evening meals, Mary opted for deep, rich hues. "It looks great in the dark," Mary says, laughing at the seeming silliness of her own remark. But she's right. The relaxed elegance of the room is cultivated by Mary's use of high-backed wicker chairs in place of more formal side chairs. The table is a simple oval without adornment. But these casual effects are juxtaposed by a spectacular Fortuny silk light fixture imported from Italy. The overall effect: a room with a special occasion feel but unimposing comfort.

$\mathcal{M}$ary's collection of Japanese lusterware packs every inch of a large dining room cabinet (facing page). Her fondness for the currently trendy china dates back to a time when it was not nearly as popular with collectors. "My first pieces were passed down from my grandmother," Mary says, "then I started seeing it around and would add pieces here and there. It used to be really cheap because no one liked it. Now, it's very hard to find and expensive," she laments. Staying true to her collecting principles, she chooses pieces based on design and finish rather than value or scarcity.

This hand-painted silk light fixture (top, right) was a rare indulgence for Mary. A few years ago, Mary encountered the art nouveau textile designs of the early twentieth-century Italian textile artist, Mariano Fortuny, at an exhibit at the Saint Louis Art Museum. The museum's shop made available light fixtures based on Fortuny's designs, and Mary just couldn't resist. Long a fan of the art nouveau style (which she employs in the border designs of much of her own artwork), Mary loves the intricate painted designs and especially the unique soft light that the lamp casts over her dining table.

pulling it all

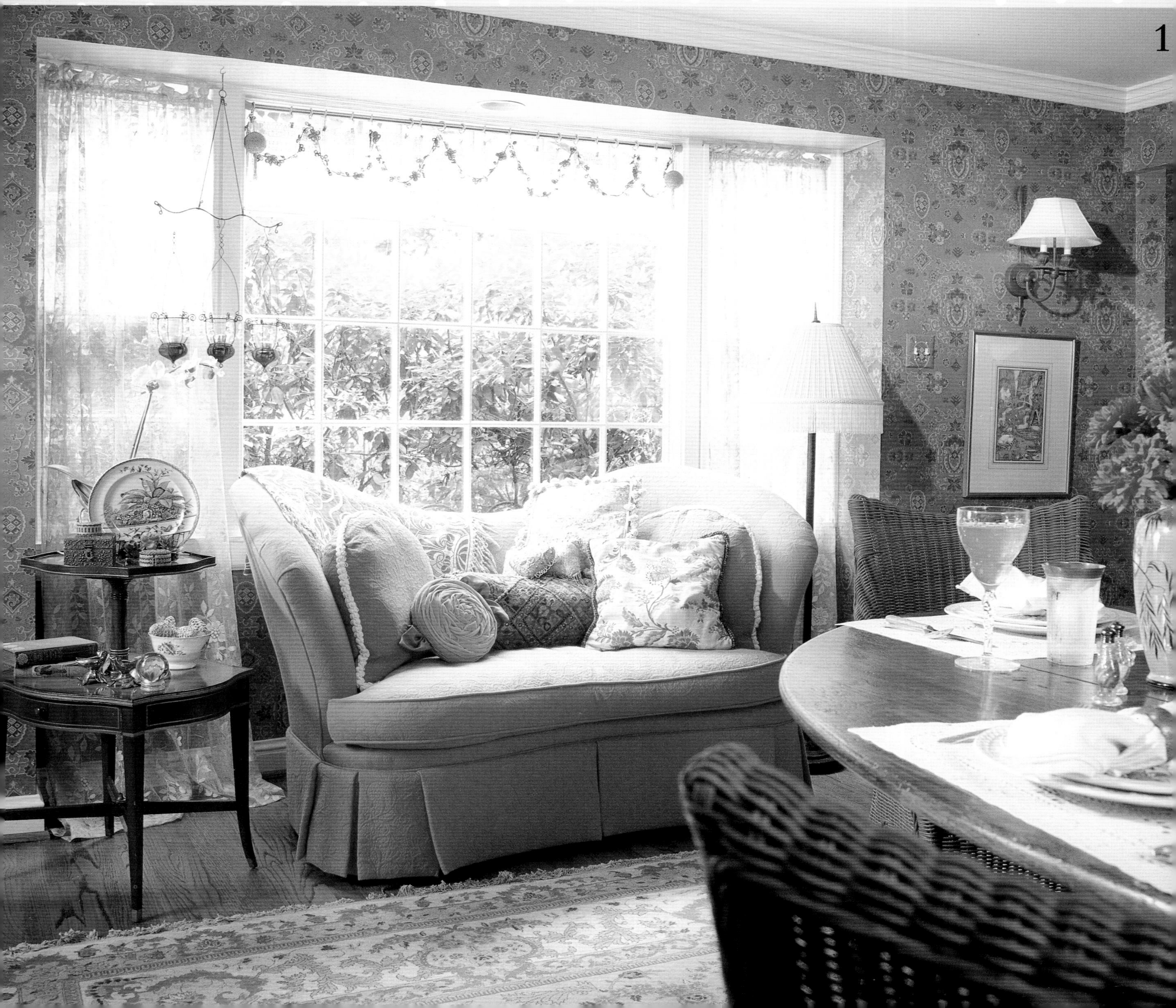

together

2

When Mary pulls a room together, it's the mix, not the match that counts. She doesn't allow herself be paralyzed by the notion that everything must fit together in a tidy and traditional way. To the contrary, she knows that points of interest—and even intrigue—are created when a fixture or furnishing provides a bit of surprise.

Mary doesn't like to lay down rules for room design—resisting even when prompted. But the Engelbreit ethos can be gleaned without too much effort. First, whenever possible, she believes in working with what she has. The hot pink settee *(1)* that now adds a shot of color to the otherwise subdued dining room last sat in the foyer of Mary's former house. Placed in this room, its role has changed completely. Though most decorators might not have seen this as a obvious fit for the room, Mary points out that pink is a natural complement to the tan and green hues of the wallpaper. Throw pillows, *(2)* side pieces, and a smattering of jewel-toned decorative items *(3)* in the dining room reassert the room's casually elegant atmosphere.

3

When she set out to redo the dining room, one of the first things Mary did was contract her friend Joseph Slattery to paint over the original multicolored French tile surrounding the fireplace (right). Using acrylics, he first laid down the wheat color, then added the vine and berry pattern, and finally painted over the grout. The tile's botanical theme is echoed by the transferware collection adorning the mantel.

The rose print above the fireplace dates from the 1920s and was purchased from a friend (opposite). It replaced an antique mirror that once hung in the same spot. On a particularly unlucky day, the massive mirror fell from the wall and shattered on the floor, wiping out several pieces of transferware on its way. Mary's lesson for the day: Always replace ancient hanging wire before hanging heavy antique wall décor!

Elegant and eclectic

When Mary sets her table (facing page), tradition is served. The silver, china, and glassware all belonged to either her paternal or maternal grandmother. The salt and pepper shakers—handblown by a local St. Louis artist—add a dash of color and contemporary styling.

This antique ballroom chair (left) is one of a pair Mary found at a favorite antique store. She loved the style and unusual gold finish, but personalized them with her own decoupage touches. As far as total furniture rehab is concerned, Mary has—for the most part—put those days behind her. "I try not to buy things that I have to commit too much time to," she says. "I don't have the patience—but I still can't resist dressing things up a bit."

Complementing the dining room's color scheme and keeping the spirit light, this quartet of prints was originally a frieze designed to decorate nursery walls (facing page). Mary found the German artwork at the Heart of the Country Antiques Show, held in Nashville.

The diminutive bird statue was an inexpensive antique store find that chirped and charmed its way into Mary's collection. "I love it," she says. "I guess because I'm a born 'nester.'"

Cozy Kitchen

Mary once said, "If my family had to depend on me for food they would starve to death in a really cute kitchen."

Visitors to Mary's home might be excused for feeling a bit displaced on the walk from the front door to the threshold of the kitchen. Up to this point, the colors have been muted, refined, understated . . . but step into Mary's kitchen and suddenly there's no doubt whose house you're in. In the hub of the home, Mary has let herself go, indulging every whim and drawing on all the trademark themes of her work: checks and cherries, hearts and cottage roses, and red, red, red!

"It's my comfort color," says Mary. "I always come back to it eventually. There's nothing else quite so warm and homey—and it truly is a neutral. It goes with every-thing in the house."

*Though the kitchen likely
would have ended up decked out
in crimson anyway, the room's primary
color was inspired by an existing accent—
the hearth in the kitchen fireplace
already sported red and white
checkerboard tiles when Mary moved in.
(Any remaining doubts that this house
was meant for this woman?)*

1

2

3

my embraceable

Few things excite Mary more than the blank canvas of a vacant room. But before deciding what furnishings, fixtures, and filigrees will go into a certain room, she first thinks about the overall atmosphere she wants to create. For Mary, the first step toward capturing a mood is choosing a color palette. Her dining room's rich browns, tans, and greens convey a slightly old-fashioned, formal air. The pale greens and creams of the living room invite a breezy, casual spirit. And in the kitchen, warm, vibrant red rules the roost. "So often, people feel paralyzed by color choices," she says. "I want my house, and this book, to convince people to relax about color. Don't worry about exact matches. Take chances. Pick out something you like—a paint color or fabric or wallpaper—and run with it. If you like the colors you're working with, you really can't go wrong."

A coterie of crimson cannisters *(facing page)* crowd a cheery watering can *(1)*. Red and gold toile shades top off tall lamps on the mantel *(2)*, while the kitchen's gingham wallpaper pulls the room together *(3)*. At right, Mary's cherry-patterned plates are right at home on the custom-made table

hues

with inlaid checks and cottage rose *(4)*. Kitchen shelves are not just for cookbooks—anything red is welcome here *(5)*.

The kitchen table (facing page), with inlaid wood checkerboard pattern and cottage rose motif, was made to Mary's specifications by a family friend, furniture maker Charlie Struckhoff.

Mary found the vintage teapot-pattern curtain years ago. She was delighted to find that it perfectly fit the kitchen's big bay window—no alteration required.

The floral pattern seat cushions on the black rattan chair were made from tablecloths.

Bright. Cheery. Slobby?

Mary jokes that the reason she and her family are so comfortable in their kitchen is that it is cute and comfortable and slobby. Though the vintage secretary (above) might seem a bit crowded, Mary keeps the critical information here (phone numbers, calendar, address book, a few favorite photos . . .) and knows where to find them. The table lamp was a candlestick that Mary had converted.

$\mathcal{M}$ary purchased the massive Arts and Crafts
cabinet at left during the kitchen redo.
One friend, Chris Herbster, painted the cabinet black
and antiqued it, and another, Claude Breckwoldt,
added the art nouveau rose motif.
The pattern is repeated on the wall cabinets
at the opposite end of the room (below).

Mary loves having a fireplace in the kitchen and plenty
of shelf space for vintage cookbooks, tins, tea sets,
and miscellanea. The unifying theme is easy to spot.
"Anything red eventually finds its way to the kitchen,"
she says with a laugh.

Transitions

A walk through Mary's house quickly reveals that her decorating magic isn't confined to the high-profile areas like the kitchen and living room. In fact, one of the greatest pleasures of a visit to Mary's is seeing how she transforms the less-obvious and out-of-the-way places: the tiny powder room off the kitchen, an upstairs hallway, the small pool house. A family room, off the kitchen, is the social center of the house.

In confined or isolated spaces like these, Mary often lets herself go a bit wild. Indeed, the secondary rooms and spaces are testament to Mary's inexhaustible drive to make every nook and cranny of this house feel like home.

Picture perfect pool parties start here
When Mary and Phil moved
into their new house, the decrepit pool house
was one of the first things to go.
"It was just rotting away," recalls Mary.
Believe it or not, this cute-as-a-button replacement
is a ready-made building
bought from a large hardware retailer—
but don't rush out to look for this model.
It has undergone some dramatic customizations
courtesy of Mary and friends.
As she says, "We cuted it up."
One look at the shutters confirms that this
one-room charmer has received
the classic Engelbreit treatment.

Books, birdhouses, boxes, and bins Decorating themes from the rest of the home spill over into the cozy confines of the cabana (facing page). Mary outfitted the room as a comfy place to take a break from the sun, stretch out with a book, or enjoy a friendly board game between dips in the pool. Mary framed vintage chinese checkers boards that she chose for their great colors and graphic appeal.

A distressed table and powder blue side chairs (above) are often moved from their usual spot on the sunporch to accommodate poolside revelry. A collection of old tin picnic hampers keep goodies within arm's reach.

Open to the early summer breeze, French doors lead from the outdoor patio and pool area to the bright and airy game room. Originally a screened-in porch, the room was enclosed by a previous owner, and now offers the perfect year-round spot for family game time.

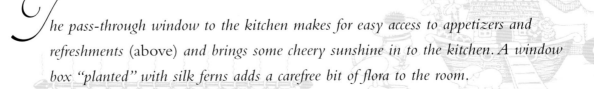

The pass-through window to the kitchen makes for easy access to appetizers and refreshments (above) and brings some cheery sunshine in to the kitchen. A window box "planted" with silk ferns adds a carefree bit of flora to the room.

Just off the crimson-hued kitchen, the butter-yellow
walls of the family room promote a relaxed mood—
although the action can heat up when a certain
preschooler is running at full steam. "Along with the
kitchen, this is where we live," says Mary. "It's the
movie-watching, puppet-show staging, story-reading,
popcorn-eating social center of the home." Mary chose
the pale yellow because she likes the way the color plays
off the reds of the adjacent kitchen. In quieter moments,
Mikayla can be found practicing her grandmother's craft
at a well-used old drawing table (above).

Don't waste time
in day dreams,
make up your mind
what to be and
begin

When you find this heart
from me,
I hope you'll very happy be,
And if you are, 'twill mean
that you
Will be my Valentine so true.

*T*he sense of refinement that characterizes Mary's home pretty much goes out the window in the downstairs powder room (affectionately referred to by residents and friends as the Valentine Bathroom). In this cozy (okay, tiny) salle de bain, Mary packs in more hearts per square inch than one would find in the mash note of a lovesick high-schooler. "It's a bit insane," Mary laughs, "but I love it. I have to have at least one room where I really cut loose." From framed, vintage valentines to tins and boxes of all sizes and design (but a singular shape) to prints of Mary's valentine themed work, there is certainly no shortage of things to look at in this effusively romantic little room. The multimedia heart collages are the work of Mary's friend, artist Linda Solovic. Perched on a painted wood vanity, the bathroom's washbowl extends the room's amorous theme. A favorite artist of Mary's, Eileen Pendergast Richardson, painted the charming basin.

Just passing through

A collection of silhouettes—some of family, others picked up secondhand—line the stairway to Mary's office (left). The two of her sons in the right-hand corner were done during a visit to Disneyland.

Every resident of Mary's home has special little extras included just for them. McKitty's silhouette isn't framed on the wall, but cut out of a door to provide easy access to a favorite room—and a little Mary whimsy at kitten height.

$\mathscr{A}$t the top of the stairs, more of Mary's vintage children's books share shelf space with miscellaneous treasures. The antique nursery stacking blocks and the very old metal teapot were both gifts from friends. The hallway's wallpaper is from the collection of designer Tracy Porter.

On a tiny shelf, not more than ten inches across, Mary has artfully arrayed a collection of items close to her heart and to her vocation.

Bedrooms

An always-on-the-go couple and an extremely energetic preschooler share this house. Peace and quiet? Serenity and solitude? Well . . . occasionally they sneak a little of those precious commodities into the average day. And when sanctuary is sought, the bedrooms are the obvious place to turn. Here we have a contrast in styles—for obvious reasons. With pale, butter-cream walls, soft lighting, and refined furnishings, the adult bedchamber is the image of calm: a place for respite and restorative sleep at the end of a hectic day.

Mikayla's room, on the other hand, is designed specifically to accommodate a hectic—and happy—day. A riot of red with gingham checked walls, a diminutive table set for tea, a menagerie of stuffed, furry friends, and whimsical touches courtesy of the Queen of Cute herself.

The winter bed

During winter months, Mary warms up
her bedroom with red linens and accents (left).
At the foot of the bed, vintage suitcases
and travel bags share space with a small display case
housing another of Mary's eye-catching vignettes.

Mary doesn't believe in keeping treasures hidden away—and family photos are no exception. The walls of her home are absolutely covered with pictures—from generations ago to last summer's vacation, no era is left undocumented or undisplayed. Amazingly, with few exceptions, these are all family pictures (both Mary's family and her husband's). For an artist whose work overflows with a sense of nostalgia, it makes perfect sense to be surrounded by such tangible and personal links to the past. And how does Mary decide what goes where? "I just start pounding nails," she says.

Soft light and a sweet yellow posy add warmth to an arrangement of family photos above the dresser in the master bedroom (1 and 2). Mary's intricate arrangements of photos leave so little bare space that wallpaper nearly becomes a redundancy. On a white wicker table in the living room (3), the freshness and innocence of childhood photos is echoed by an arrangement of lily of the valley and a small soapstone angel figurine.

102

treasures

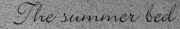

The summer bed

With a change of linens and a few accent pieces, the master bedroom is transformed from winter
warmth to summer sunlight. Mary first changed the color scheme of her bedding after a trip to
Florida, having been inspired by the strong light and pale palette of the seashore.

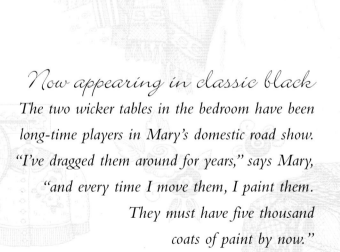

Now appearing in classic black
The two wicker tables in the bedroom have been
long-time players in Mary's domestic road show.
"I've dragged them around for years," says Mary,
"and every time I move them, I paint them.
They must have five thousand
coats of paint by now."

Lavishing the lavatory

Just off the master bedroom, Mary's bathroom bears her distinctive touch—even in the most unlikely places. She decoupaged the medicine cabinet (opposite and lower right) in an all-night burst of inspiration. "I wanted something nice to look at every morning and every night," she explains matter-of-factly. Among towels (below) and "other useful things," Mary has assembled the usual suspects: framed photos, vintage books, boxes, and tins, and a bell jar display she designed specifically for the bathroom.

How quickly they grow In the time between two photo-shoots for this book, Mikayla had graduated from crib (page 110) to big-girl bed (opposite). The quilt is an antique store find. Either way, the room is any little girl's dream room.

A sense of history helps color Mikayla's room, though she doesn't know it yet. The five-drawer dresser (above) belonged to Mary's uncle when he was a boy. Mary, of course, added a coat of paint and a dose of decoupage. "It's been painted many, many times," she admits.

Mary created the hat gift box valance and painted and decoupaged the tot-sized tea table especially for Mikayla's room. Framed illustrations (her own and others') add sugar and spice to the gingham-patterned walls.

Tea sets, toy storks, and no end of tiny treasures take up residence in a built-in cabinet in Mikayla's room (opposite). The tea set collection includes some old, some new, and some designed by Mary herself.

Perched on a shelf above the door, a (small) portion of Mary's long-standing monkey collection keeps watch over Mikayla's room—where monkeying around is strongly encouraged—except at bed time (below)!

McKitty waits for teatime (right). (The cat's name was a compromise—Mikayla originally wanted to name her kitten "Mikayla.")

$\mathcal{M}$ary's stork collection (left) *started with the birth of her second son, Mikayla's uncle Will.*

The heart collage on Mikayla's wall (below) is destined to be passed down through generations, too. It was created by Mary's friend, artist Linda Solovic.

*T*he darling dress hanging on Mikayla's wall was originally made from a tablecloth and has made the rounds with Mary for a long time. She bought it at an antique store when her sons were small. After all these years, it's finally found the perfect home.

Studio

The last stop on our tour of Mary's home is the spot where she usually ends her day (which is typically well after most people end theirs). Mary is a night owl—and her studio is her nest, perched high above the living space of the rest of the house.

The room that houses Mary's studio is the result of the only major renovation that the family has made to the house. Where once was a lofty two-story entry to the home, they lowered the ceiling to normal height, freeing up a cozy attic space for Mary's drawing table, flat files, supplies, and even a little nook with a guest bed. The studio is literally tucked into the rafters of the house, with sloped walls that follow the roofline. It is a bit cramped and a trifle cluttered, but a cozy and quiet spot where Mary can be alone with her thoughts and her work.

In her element
Mary tucks in among glasses
of colored pencils, bowls of paint,
and buckets of markers.
She starts a new design in
pencil, eventually filling it in
with marker. On her desk now?
A new illustration for her wall
calendar (facing page).

Tools of her trade and sources of inspiration surround her. A cadre of quaintly futuristic little metal robots stands sentry at the edge of her drawing table. A box of bowties here . . . a jar of buttons there . . . and pictures—more family pictures—are every-where. Mary never knows when one of these little mementos will ignite the creative spark that might become her next drawing.

And her greatest (and most distracting) source of inspiration is often close at hand—and underfoot—as well. Mikayla loves to be with Mary when she works, and Mary draws endless ideas from the words and deeds of her little apprentice. For the most part, Mary takes a hands-off approach to Mikayla's work. "I teach a little," she says, "but encourage a lot. She has definitely reawak-ened feelings in me that I haven't felt since my boys were little," Mary says. "And that does find its way into my drawings—a lot."

Safely under glass
Old postcards, stamps, and an
assortment of family photos add
texture and depth to a small side
table in Mary's studio (right).

The downside is that Mary finds it nearly impossible to work when her little assistant is fiddling about. Hers is, after all, a delicate business requiring considerable concentration. Still, Mary doesn't like to deny Mikayla access to any part of the house. Her solution? She's recently dragged a child's drawing table out of storage—the same one in fact that she herself used when she was a little girl. (Do you get the impression that Mary has never gotten rid of anything in her life? You wouldn't be far off.) The little table now sits not far from Mary's own and while Mikayla colors away, Mary is able to steal a few uninterrupted minutes to work.

On most days, though, Mary doesn't sit down at her table until after the rest of the household has settled in for the night. After a typical day that might include review of product prototypes, meetings with staff at her company, household errands, and lots and lots of playtime, pretend time, snack times, and story times with her granddaughter—after McKitty is fed and Mikayla's in bed . . . only then does Mary pick up the pencils.

Ready reference Mary keeps a large library of art and design books close at hand in her studio (opposite). "I still haven't got this drawing thing down," she jokes. "I use them all the time." The file boxes hold stickers, decoupage materials, and other tidbits Mary uses for work and play. Large flat files (above) hold paper, stationery, and other pretty parchments that help get the creative juices flowing.

1

2

3

playtime

There's an undefinable something about Mary Engelbreit's artwork that makes it unique and resonant; a sense of nostalgia and winsomeness that can't be manufactured or faked. This Engelbreit magic manifests itself on her drawing table, but it doesn't start here. It started long ago, when Mary was a little, pigtailed girl drinking in the wide world with wondering eyes. The little girl is now a grandmother, but still, somehow, retains an open link to the past. How does she gain such ready access to those simpler times? Well, for one, she has amazingly clear memories of her own childhood. She also surrounds herself with mementos of those bygone days. The old storybooks, toys, dolls, and games, the robots and monkeys—they all have the ability to trigger ideas in Mary, ideas that translate into artwork that connects people with things they didn't realize they still remembered. Mary knows that there's power in playthings and she'll always make room in her house for more. *(1)* Vintage ceramic circus figures await arrangement in a shadow box.

(2) Buttons, bowties, and family snapshots crowd a studio side table. *(3)* All manner of minis fill a printer's shelf. *(4 and 5)* Mary is a prodigious clipper and collector . . . because you just never know what might inspire next.

Tucked into the rafters

An antique brass daybed and overstuffed
chair turn this little attic nook into cozy
guest quarters. On nights when a busy
mind (or an impending deadline) keep
Mary working late, she occasionally makes
use of the bed to catch at least a few hours
of well-earned sleep.

Heartsease and hardwood Looking for all the world like it was plucked from one of Mary's illustrations, this little side chair was another fortuitous flea market find. It sits in the little nook outside Mary's studio. The Scottie seat cushion was a gift from a friend who obviously knows Mary well.

$\mathcal{M}$ary began collecting toy robots—some old, some new—when her sons were young, but admits that it was as much for her as for them. "I decorated their room with robots," she says, "pretending to myself that they wanted them. They did like them, but they liked the newer ones that could do things. I only like the old-fashioned ones."

" . . . Ultimately, a house is just a house.
What's important is what you do in it."

Epilogue

Honeymoons can't last forever. So, after five years of living in the house that she had coveted for so long, does it still hold the same allure as when she first glimpsed it through the trees nearly two decades ago? On this point, Mary turns a bit philosophical. "Well, ultimately, a house is just a house," she says. "What's important is what you do in it. That's what makes it a home. You definitely associate different periods of your life with the house you live in. We lived in a really cute house in Webster when my boys were little, and for that reason I will always cherish memories of that house. I know that that's the house they would think of as home."

"But there is something
about this house," she continues.
"It's different.
I've loved it for so long,
and somehow it just looks and feels
the most like me—
the most like I always imagined
my house would look."

In the five years they've lived in the house, Mary has redone virtually every room. Cosmetically, the house has very little in common with the one they inherited. They've also made some needed improvements to the exterior—including a new roof and new exterior paint. But Mary and Phil have been intentionally deliberate about making significant changes and renovations. They wanted to live with the house for a while before seriously digging in.

quarters or a more spacious bedroom for Mikayla when she's older and needs more room to roam. She's also been dreaming about building a second-story sleeping porch adjacent to her and Phil's bedroom. This would be built above what is now the game room downstairs—which, incidentally, she's thinking about turning into an exercise room. Except for when she's thinking about converting it back into a screened-in porch.

"I'll walk by something—a lamp or table or curtain—and think, 'hmm . . . what can I do to help that? How can I make that look better?'"

By now, however, Mary has a pretty clear plan on what she'd like to do next. She's been giving a lot of thought to the home's little-used third floor. She'd like to add dormers to the roof and turn the entire floor into guest

As is the norm in Mary's world, the ideas keep coming, and plans are subject to change.

As for the décor in her home, well, that's never entirely a *fait accompli*. Mary will forever be a tinkerer and a tweaker. It's not unusual

for her to walk through a room that she's walked through hundreds of times and suddenly be stopped in her tracks. "I'll walk by something—a lamp or table or curtain—and think, 'hmm . . . what can I do to help that? How can I make that look better?' " And she admits that sometimes the changes are more wholesale in nature. She's already pulled

off major redos of Mikayla's room, her own bedroom, and the living room; changing color schemes, rearranging or swapping out furniture, putting up new wallpaper . . . no room

in Mary's house is ever really placed in the "finished" column.

Mary realizes that her home might be something of a revelation to her fans. It isn't all checks and cherries. Not by a long shot. "When the magazine *(Mary Engelbreit's Home Companion)* publishes pictures of my house, people invariably say, 'But it doesn't look like you.' Well, I do understand why they would say that, but every room can't be in the same color palette and scream out 'Mary Engelbreit' in the traditional sense—with checks, cherries, hearts, Scotties, and black, white, and red. I mean, I still love those elements—just look in my bathroom and kitchen—but I don't want that all over the place. It would wear you out. And the fact is that all of these other things are me, too. It's just a more subtle approach."

Indeed, every room in Mary's house—from the pale, sunny, seashore-inspired living room to the darker, understated dining room—bears the underpinnings, however subtle, of Mary's unique and immediately identifiable vision. The nostalgic character,

the playfulness, the birdcages and bell jars, the old family photos, the mixing of high and low design elements, the prominence of collections . . . all of these things are as much "Mary" as a cottage rose or checkerboard tile. They are just, perhaps, not as obvious. And that's precisely what Mary likes about them.

some way to make it a little more like that private vision in her head—the vision of what the perfect home should be. Will this house be the final picture in Mary's long-running book of much-loved homes—wood smoke curling lazily up from the chimney above a steep-pitched roof?

"Mary knows that this storybook story is far from over.
Every day in this house that she's loved for so long,
she sees some way to make it a little more like
that private vision in her head—
the vision of what the perfect home should be."

As long as an artist keeps dreaming, her work is never done. And as much as she loves a happy ending, Mary knows that this story-book story is far from over. Every day in this house that she's loved for so long, she sees

As for Mary, she doesn't honestly know and wouldn't want to. After all, the best part about any story is not knowing how it turns out.

Happy? Yes. Ending? Only time will tell . . . .

Credits

*M*any people made this book possible, including the hardworking staffs
at Andrews McMeel Publishing and Mary Engelbreit Studios,
especially David Arnold who helped get us out of a pinch with some great ideas.

All the photographs are copyright John Gould Bessler,
with the exception of the photos on the following pages:

pages 98, 110, 112 copyright Matthew Millman
pages 49, 53 copyright Gordon Beall
pages 4, 35, 39, 42, 57, 58, 59, 62, 66, 67, 68, 77, 79, 90, 102 copyright Barbara Martin

Thanks to *Mary Engelbreit's Home Companion Magazine* for helping us round out
our pictures of Mary's house with the help of Matthew, Gordon, and especially Barbara.

Many thanks to Linda McCrary for letting us use her beautiful watercolor of Mary's house
on the endpapers and occasionally throughout the book.

Special thanks to stylist Heidi Adams for her finishing touches
and writer Patrick Regan for bringing Mary's story to life! She adores you both.

Designer Stephanie R. Farley,
who has been designing Mary Engelbreit books for over ten years,
pulled out all the stops for this book and made it look easy.

—*Polly Blair,* Editor

There is music in the word home.
To the old it brings a bewitching strain
from the harp of memory;
to the young it is a reminder of all that
is near and dear to them.
Amoung the many songs
we are wont to listen to,
there is not one more cherished
than the touching melody of
"Home, Sweet Home."

—D. H. Wever (The Mother's Legacy, *1908)*